A NEW

LIFE

By
Steve & Amy Willis

Daystar Publishing
P.O. Box 464
Miamitown, Ohio 45041

All Scripture is taken from
The King James Bible

ISBN 978-1-890120-84-9

Printed by
Instant Publisher

Table of Contents

~ ~ ~ ~ ~ ~ ~ ~

INTRODUCTION

INDIVIDUAL STORIES

THE WAY OF SALVATION

INTRODUCTION

The following are stories of individuals who found the answer to the ever-consuming question:

WHERE WILL I GO WHEN I DIE?

These stories tell how they came to the understanding that they really were not headed for heaven, but were actually on their way to hell. They then realized that they needed to find God's way of going to Heaven. Some individuals were religious, others were not, but the basis for salvation is the same for all people. Here are the stories of the transformation that took place in their hearts that changed their lives completely.

Individual Stories

*But sanctify the Lord God in your hearts: and
be ready always to give an answer to every man
that asketh you a reason of the hope that
is in you with meekness and fear.*
I Peter 3:15

*And they overcame him by the blood of the
Lamb, and by the word of their testimony;
and they loved not their lives unto the death.*
Revelation 12:11

CYNTHIA RUBY

I came from a Navy family. We moved up and down the East Coast several times within my Father's 23 years of enlistment. My three brothers and I were all born in different States.

My mother told us that we didn't go to church because we weren't in one place long enough to attend. I believed her. We didn't know any differently.

One day in 1968, my father came home and told us that he was leaving the Navy and moving one more time. This time to Pascagoula, Mississippi. Within three months, we moved to the bayou of Southern Mississippi. It was very different than any Naval Station we had been to, but it was home for my dad.

The next year, I turned thirteen. That summer, my older brother brought over a new friend he had met. His name was James Cook. He was one of the nicest guys I had ever met. As we were all sitting outside, he came across the front porch and sat beside me. With a quiet voice, he asked, "Cindy would you like to come to church with me this Sunday?"

It was the first time anyone had ever asked me to go to church. I said, "Yes". After he had left, I asked my mom if we were going to stay there long enough to go to church. She said "Yes". That Sunday my older brother and I went to Arlington Heights Baptist Church. We went for a couple of weeks and then attended VBS (Vacation Bible School), for one week.

The Sunday after VBS, I was sitting in a morning service and the Lord drew me to the point where I saw myself as God saw me. I remember thinking that I was a good girl and obeyed my parents and did things right, but that morning, I became very embarrassed before God.

When the invitation was given, the pastor reminded us that Hell was awaiting those who denied the free gift of salvation. I knew in my heart that if I did not respond, I would be denying the opportunity to be saved.

At first, I didn't go forward, then the pastor said, "This verse is for you, let go, and let me introduce you to Jesus Christ." As people were singing, I let go and walked straight to Pastor Wisser and told him that I was lost and going to Hell. I had never before heard of salvation or the reality of Jesus Christ or Hell. Pastor Wisser asked me some questions to make sure I understood who Jesus Christ was and what He did for me. I don't know how I understood, but the Lord showed me my state and I knew what I had to do. That morning, I received the Lord Jesus Christ into my heart. My life changed directions from that point on.

Although later, there was a time when I was without a church again, the Lord never left me. It wasn't until after I was married, that I began attending church again. Here it was that I began to grow in the Lord. I praise God for a church that teaches the Bible faithfully.

RACHELLE EVANS

I was raised in a very Catholic home.

When I was in third or fourth grade, my catechism teacher taught us that we sinned in thought, word and deed. She told us that when we went to confession, the priest would absolve our sins and we would be forgiven. She explained that our soul was like a circle and whenever we would sin, it would get black dots on it. She further said that if we died when we had black dots on our soul, we would go to hell. By confessing our sins and being absolved, the black dots would be washed away. With this in mind, I faithfully went to confession. Yet, even as a child, I knew that as soon as I got home, I would sin again. I often wondered how anyone could ever get to heaven, since we sin so easily. I would even pray that I would die right after I went to confession before I had a chance to sin again.

Even though I was a very good Catholic, by the time I graduated from high school, I quit going to confession and the church, because I didn't see how I could ever be good enough to go to heaven. I figured that I was going to go hell anyway, because I couldn't keep from sinning. Although I was a rather good girl, my main struggle was thinking bad thoughts about other people .

I later got married and my husband was a Lutheran. He didn't want to become Catholic, so we would go to the Lutheran church once in a while. It didn't matter to me. It seemed like it was always the same thing, and often after the service, my husband would say, "There was another wasted hour!"

I started working at the Post Office. There I met a man who really knew the Bible and was constantly talking to me about it. One day, we went out for coffee and he asked me, "If you were to die today, would you go to heaven or hell?" I answered, "Hell". He was a little surprised, since most people think and hope that they will go to heaven. But I knew what sin was and that I couldn't stop from sinning. He then asked me if I wanted to go to heaven. Of course I wanted to go! I would have done anything in order to go!!! Then he showed me, from the Bible, how to be saved and go to heaven. I believed all that he said and ended up praying and asking God to forgive me and save me. He then told me that I was "saved", but nothing had happened in my heart.

I kept seeing him at work and he would continually tell me that since I was saved, I should go to church that taught the Bible. Finally, one Sunday, I went to his church. During the preaching, I wondered how the Preacher seemingly knew so much about me. I knew that what he spoke on about salvation, I didn't have. By the end of the service, my hands were shaking so badly that I never wanted to go back again.

All that week, I thought about what that Preacher said, and I knew everything was true. I thought maybe I would try and go back again just to see if it was the same as the first time. I was also confused about salvation, because if I already did what you're supposed to do, in order to be saved, then how could I get saved again?

I did go back and again I was very uncomfortable, and knew I did not have what they called salvation.

One day, my friend brought me a book to read called, *The Dark Side of Calvary*, by Al Lacy. I took it and began to read it. It was about Jesus' death on the cross. When I got to the part where it talked about Jesus drinking the bitter cup of our sin, it was as if God said, *"Rachelle, you killed Jesus Christ with your sins. It was your sins first that entered Him."*

Then the light broke through and for the first time, I realized it wasn't the Roman soldiers that killed Jesus, it was **MY** sin. Before, I did not know anything about Jesus, but now I understood the price that Jesus had paid. Now it was personal.

Before, I had just wanted to go to heaven for myself, now I realized what salvation was all about. I then bowed my head and in repentance, I asked God to save me.

From then, my life totally changed. I was shocked. God put a thirst in my heart to learn more about Him. I went to church with an eagerness that was not my own. I finally had my sins forgiven forever, and I am so thankful.

RUSS HOVENDICK

When I was growing up, I attended the Lutheran church and fulfilled all of the requirements. I was baptized as a baby, attended church and Sunday School faithfully, and was confirmed in the ninth grade.

I remember having a discussion with my Lutheran minister when I was getting ready to be confirmed. I told him that I was really scared of dying and going to hell. He told me that I had nothing to fear, because my sins were washed away at my baptism, and I was faithful in attendance and that I would be confirmed. All I needed to do now, was to live the best life possible. Even with those words, I wasn't satisfied and still had a deep down concern for my soul.

Since I was raised on a farm, I listened to the tractor radio a lot. On occasion, I would listen to preachers that talked about repentance and faith in Jesus being the only way to Heaven. Once again, thoughts of dying, and not knowing where I would go, bothered me.

In the mid 1970's, I was working for 3-M in Hutchinson, MN and befriended a guy who asked me to breakfast one morning. During breakfast, he asked a very simple but troubling question, *"If you died today do you know where you would go?"* I told him that no one could know for sure, but that I was baptized, confirmed, and trying to live a good life.

He then showed me what the Bible says about salvation and knowing your eternal destiny. Later, I left the position with 3-M and never saw that man again. But although

I tried to put those thoughts away, they troubled me.

Different times I would think about dying and a deep down sick feeling would possess me. When these feelings came, I tried to hide them by having fun partying. Still, there was this emptiness that I could not explain.

In 1979, I married my wife and believed, that would fill the void that I had been experiencing. It didn't, and I continued to party. Finally, I started to read the Bible and search for answers. God then began to really deal with my heart. One night, I woke up in a sweat, frightened, and my heart was pounding. My wife wanted to know what was wrong, and I told her that I believed if I died, I would go to hell. That was the first time, I admitted what I really knew and believed. She advised me to go see my pastor, who had said, I had nothing to worry about, since I was doing all the right things. This did not comfort me.

I then decided to call my brother, who had written and told me that he had accepted Christ. That weekend, I drove 4 hours to meet with him. He brought out the Bible and showed me that I was already condemned - had sinned against God because I was a sinner and deserved hell. We talked all night until 6 a.m., still, I was not convinced and went to bed.

At 9 that morning, we went to see a preacher who, again, showed me from the Bible that I was a sinner and had to repent and accept Jesus as Lord. I needed to trust Him to do all the saving. Finally, I realized that there was nothing I could do to earn eternal life, and I accepted Christ that day in May, 1980. I experienced a peace that overflowed in my soul!!

Since then, I had an hunger for God's Word, and God has given me a direction and purpose to my. He has also given me what man and religion could not give me: the wonderful assurance that when I die, I will spend eternity in Heaven.

LISA MARIE PHILLIPS

I did not really have a religious background growing up. My parents attended a Methodist church until I was 3 years old. Then, when I was 4, my parents divorced. A year later, my mother re-married. My new stepfather was a Catholic, so once in a while we would attend Mass. All I remember was that it was horribly boring. Later, when I was a teenager, I attended a service at a Southern Baptist Church with a friend, but no one shared the gospel with me.

Around 17, my mother moved to Aberdeen, SD to be with her fourth husband, and my sister and I went to live with my father. Before she left, my mother told me to make sure to get baptized. I was shocked! She had never mentioned anything about religion before. I never gave a thought before about eternal matters until she made that statement to me. This is where my journey to eternal life began.

I began thinking about the end of the world, because that would include me. Since I was still young, I did not think that I would die anytime soon, but if the whole world came to an end, then I would be included in that scenario. I was scared and remember crying a lot out of fear. I would pray every night before bed. Because I didn't know how to pray, I would pray a repetition I had learned. *"Now, I lay me down to sleep, I pray the Lord my soul, to keep...."* This did not lead to the salvation of my soul, but it was an attempt to obtain forgiveness. I had not heard of the Saviour and his saving grace.

I remember visiting my mother in Aberdeen and I was crying before bed, afraid of hell. My mother told me that I was a good person, and that God will take me to heaven. But her words did not comfort me. Even at the young age of 17, I knew that I had too many sins, and that I was not such a good person. I am glad that I did not accept my mother's words or I would be destined for a devil's hell.

Three years went by. I was 20 and a drunk. I worked 2nd shift at a factory and my friends started to drop off. They didn't want to wait for me to get off work, which ended up a good thing for me. I felt really rejected and decided to clean up. I quit drinking, started exercising and eating better. I soon became very lonely and depressed. I was working at a factory and had no future.

Soon after this, God started working on me again. I was under heavy conviction and cried out to God and asked Him if I could ever be forgiven. I remember asking him what I could do to make things right. Then I tried to make things right on my own. A while back, I had stolen a bike when I was drunk to use as transportation, so I rode that bike in very cold weather and returned it. I ended up getting sick as a result. I soon realized that I could not undo all of the sins I had committed, and was convinced that there was nothing I could do to make things right.

I started visiting a Christian Reformed church in town with my sisters-in-laws. I even asked the Pastor what I could do to go to heaven, and whether I needed to get baptized. He was very cold to me and just gave me a booklet for confirmation or something. I worked on it at home, but didn't know most of the answers (it was a fill in the blank booklet). I was very discouraged.

Then in April of 1997, I got the best invitation of my life. A lady invited my sisters-in-laws to her church. They knew I was searching for the truth, so they asked me if I wanted to go with them to this Baptist church. I happily went.

When I visited this Independent Baptist Church in town, the pastor said that the Bible tells how to know for sure that you will go to heaven. I was under heavy conviction, but at the invitation time to go forward, and have someone show me how to be saved, my feet did not move. I stood and cried. I am glad the Lord is longsuffering and gave me another chance.

I came back to visit the next week. I just couldn't wait. Same thing happened at the end of the service. The pastor said if you don't know where you will spend eternity, we can show you from the Bible how you can be saved and have a home in heaven. I stood and cried, but again I did not move. This time, my sister's mother-in-law, told her to ask me if I wanted to go. I was happy to go , thank God all it took was a person to ask me. I went almost running up to the alter, crying.

The pastor's wife opened her Bible and showed me how I could have a home in heaven. I simply placed all of my faith in Jesus as my only hope and I called on him to save me. The verse I remember best was Romans 10:13. *"For whosoever shall call upon the name of the Lord shall be saved."* The pastor's wife helped me to pray. When I stood up, I had such peace and joy. I was gloriously saved. I knew that my sins were forgiven and I was on my way to heaven.

Two-weeks later I was baptized in full immersion as the Bible teaches and became am member. I learned that you place all of your trust in Christ for salvation and then you get baptized. Baptism has no connection with salvation, but is done in obedience to Christ; it pictures his death, burial and resurrection.

The Bible taught me that there was nothing I could do of myself to gain heaven. The Bible also taught me that I could not work for heaven, that Jesus did the work when he died on the cross, was buried and then rose again three days later. It is his blood that pays the price for the sins of all who will trust in his finished work. *"Now to him that worketh is the reward not reckoned of grace, but of dept. But to him that worketh not, but believeth on him that justifieth the ungodly, his faith is counted for righteousness."* Romans 4:4,5

I thank the Lord that there was someone to show me the way of righteousness and how I could become a child of God and have eternal life.

REV. DAVID LEE

God allowed me to be born in a Christian home where the Bible was read and taught. There was prayer before meals, and we went to church three times a week. My family was large and I was the fourth of six children.

We lived in a small town and attended the Assemblies of God church. We were well respected as a godly Christian family. That was in the early 50's and without the influence of the worldly things of our modern culture. Yet, our home was full of hypocrisy.

I had lots of friends at church and we had a grand time answering Bible questions, and memorizing verses. There were Sunday School outings to Bro. Bob's farm, and hay rides at the Tanner's place, and the annual Sunday School picnic with games and contests. We had lots of clean fun.

Then something happened in our home that gave rise to great sorrow and tragedy. My mom and dad decided to get a TV. We, as a family, made a commitment that we would always turn off the beer and cigarette commercials and that we would not watch it at all on the Lord's day. With these things agreed to, we thought that most of the destructive influence would be neutralized. So in it came! There was Sky King, Laurel and Hardy, Mickey Mouse and Loony Tunes. At first we still read the Bible before bed time, but it was not long until our affection for the Word of God was in bad repair. Then Mom started watching the soap operas.

Finally, when I was about 13, Dad and Mom announced that they were getting a divorce. I was totally devastated. I remember watching my dad load up his car and back out of the drive way, and head down the street. Tears filled my eyes, and I ran to the tree-house that Dad had built for me and cried and cried until I could not cry any more.

Back then, it was a shame to get a divorce. So I started missing Sunday School. Neither our pastor nor my S.S. teachers visited us. It was like no one really cared.

"Besides," I thought. "If God couldn't keep our family together there must not be a whole lot to this Christianity business anyway."

As a teenager, "Nobody cares, nobody cares! Why should I care!", kept going through my mind.

Years went by, then in 1969, I found myself married with one daughter and another on the way. I was working in the same factory that my dad had worked for years. I wanted my dad's friendship so when he asked me to meet him for supper at work, I was greatly pleased.

At those suppertime encounters, my dad would greet me with a hug and kiss. He would pray for our food and as I ate he would read to me the Bible. I felt that I had been set-up.

God used my dad to bring to memory all the Scriptures I had learned as a boy. The Lord began to work on my heart and I began to wonder:

Why was I here on this earth?

Where had I come from?

Where was I going?

Is this all there is to life: to eat, sleep, work and die?

God began to bring conviction to my soul concerning my sin. Oh, I remember praying as a child and asking Jesus to save me, but it was without true understanding and repentance.

I knew what I should do, but I kept putting God off.

Then one day while driving to work, God spoke to my heart. It was like He said to me, "Either you get saved TODAY or you never will!" While at work, that was all I could think of.

As I drove home that night, these thoughts intensified. My wife was asleep in bed. I knelt down by the bedside and began to pray and ask the Lord to save me. Being raised in a Pentecostal church, I had pre-conceived ideas of how it would be when I got saved. None of these things happened, so I thought that God was gone and He was not going to save me.

The only thing I knew was to get my Bible and open it to the book of Romans. I read chapter ten carefully.

> *That if thou shalt confess with thy mouth the*
> *Lord Jesus, and shalt believe in thine heart that*
> *God hath raised him from the dead, thou shalt be*
> *saved. . . . for whosoever shall call upon the name*
> *of the Lord shall be saved.*

Then I prayed. This time it was different. I told the Lord that I was a sinner, and that I was fully aware of the fact that He would be perfectly just to send me to hell forever. I said,

"Lord, I don't know how to ask you any more sincerely than I am asking you. You said if I believed with the heart that I would not be ashamed of you. As best as I know how, I am going to confess you to others. I know that I can't change my life, but that you can change me. Now, Lord I have asked you to save me. That is your promise. You cannot lie. You are my only hope of heaven. Thank- you Jesus for saving me."

I got up from my knees and went to bed. There were not any bells, nor did I speak in tongues, but there was a settled peace in my heart that God had saved me.

Morning came and I looked at the night stand. There were the cigarettes. I had been smoking two packs a day. I bowed my head and asked God to take them away from me.

Praise God! He did! I haven't had another to this day.

At work, I asked God to give me strength to confess Him before my co-workers. A few weeks before, a man I was working with had asked me if I believed like my old man. I had told him, "NO! I don't believe any of that junk!" That day, I asked him, "You remember when you asked me if I believed like my dad?"

"Sure." he said.

"Well, I believe just like my dad, now. Last night I received Christ as my Saviour and I'm on my way to Heaven." I answered.

He cocked his head and bellowed a laugh. "You're crazy Lee."

I answered, "Well, if I am, then I'm the happiest crazy person you've ever seen".

And I still am!

DONNA LEE

As far back as I can remember, my mother always took my brother and I to Sunday School at a United Brethren church. As a young girl, I did not give much thought to God or the Bible except for Sunday mornings. It seemed like we put on our Christianity, just as we put on special clothes for church. Therefore, I saw no relationship between God and my everyday life. He had His place in that little slot on Sundays and that was all.

There was one godly influence in our family. That was my grandfather. He truly loved the Lord, His Word and talking to the Lord in prayer. He was the only one I knew that actually prayed outside of the church building.

When I was in seventh grade, my grandfather died. I was devastated. One Sunday afternoon, I was discouraged and wanted to know the true purpose and meaning of life. I had been crying since the morning service. My mom called the Preacher and he came to our house. I clearly remember him going through God's Four Spiritual laws:

1. God loves you and offers a wonderful plan for your life. (Jn. 3:16).
2. Man is sinful and separated from God. (Rom. 3:23)
3. Jesus Christ is God's only provision for man's sin. (Rom. 5:8)
4. We must individually receive Christ as Saviour and Lord. (Jn. 1:12)

He then told me that I could right now receive Christ by faith. So I prayed a suggested prayer.

I thought that I had really meant that prayer and did "feel better" for a short while. I tried reading the Bible and being good, but I continually failed. I was not free from the law of sin and death. I had been taught that one had to be good enough to keep their salvation, and I clearly was not good enough. After a while, I gave up trying to live the Christian life and hoped that when I was too old to sin anymore, the Lord would give me a chance to receive Christ before I died.

I continued going to church with my mother until I graduated from High School. Then, I totally went my own way, not giving God much thought. I had met David Lee when I was about fifteen, and after High School, we became "steady dates" and soon married. I thought we would live happily-ever-after. This was what I wanted; a wonderful husband, a nice little home, and a family. I thought this would bring fulfillment to my life and contentment to my heart. I put myself totally into our marriage.

For a few years, things went well. I loved being a wife and mother. Then God started to unsettle things. When I was expecting our second child, I once again began to wonder,

What is the purpose of my existence? Am I here on earth to keep my house clean, my husband happy, and train our child? Train her for what? To some day be able to keep her house clean, her husband happy and train her children? There has to be more to life than that!!

Around this time, I also had a real desire to go back to church. Though I did not realize it, my heart was lonely for God. My husband was also under conviction and we began to be a little edgy. I did not like my secure world being disrupted nor my marriage unhappy. One afternoon, I asked my husband, "What's wrong with us?" He replied, "I don't know about you, but I'm under conviction!" I was surprised that he was even thinking about God.

A few days later, my husband told me that he had trusted Christ as his Saviour. I wondered, "OK, but what does that mean? What will that mean to our home?" I just had to see what this was all about.

We began going to church three times a week. He began tithing and we had prayer before meals and at bedtime. We did not have the same friends over on Saturday night, and he did not drink anymore. He even changed to some "weird" music instead of our normal Rock. He then began reading the Bible to me! Wow, this was really different. It was as if God was a part of our life, not just a Sunday church God. I wondered if it was real and if it would last.

After several weeks of living with my husband being such a different person, I began to be thirsty for God. All the Scripture that had been in my heart as a young girl was now being watered. I fell on my knees and repented of my sin, self-will and rebellion and yielded my stubborn will to the Lord.

What a difference from the first time I had asked Him to be my Saviour. Now, He really was! The Scriptures were alive and Christ brought a contentment to my troubled heart. What joy filled my soul! He was REAL in my heart and life! My life changed immediately.

RYAN THOMPSON

I was introduced to the need of salvation by a co-worker at Royal Fork. His name was Jeff Blust.

I had just graduated from high school and was working part-time at Royal Fork while planning to attend college at USD in the Fall. It was during that summer that Jeff introduced me to my need of salvation.

I can remember standing out in the parking lot, one summer night after work, with another fellow visiting with Jeff. He asked us if we heard about man's inherited sin nature, or something like that. This was the first time I had ever heard that I was a born sinner, because I had inherited it all the way back from Adam. This made me feel a little uneasy, because nobody had said things to me like Jeff did that night. I really thought about what he was saying and it troubled me.

It was later in the summer that Jeff confronted me again as we sat in a booth. He preached quite a bit and told me that I needed to be saved and that only God could save me. Some things he said were very offensive, but I knew he was telling me the truth.

Finally in the Fall, I escaped from his preaching and went to college. Then during Christmas break, I came home and went to work for a couple of weeks. Of course, Jeff was there. He asked me how my soul was doing, and I responded much nicer than I felt. I wanted to tell him to "Get off my back" or "Shut up! I'm tired of hearing all this about how I need to be saved!"

At the end of the shift, Jeff came back to the dish room and just hammered away at me. He explained his salvation and how he was living for Christ. This really started to bother me inside. I couldn't argue with what he was saying because I knew that it was true. I wondered, "What am I supposed to do?" I knew I needed to be saved, so I told him that I would go to church with him on Sunday. I kept my word and am glad for it.

That Sunday, I met Jeff at church and sat with him through the service. What a service it was! I don't remember all that was preached, but I know the Lord literally stirred my heart to no end! During the invitation, I believed in my heart and repented and trusted Christ as my Lord and Saviour. At that moment, I was born-again. That was Jan 5, 1997, the greatest day of my life.

DAVID THOMPSON

It all started in February of 1997, after my brother, Ryan, got saved. I was downstairs razzing him about going to this church of his. He had never gone to church so much before, so I asked him if he was following marriage requirements in order to marry a lady in this church. He emphatically said, "NO!" and I just laughed it off wondering what did he get himself into. My mother and I talked about it and thought it was just a fad he was going through.

It was around this time, I began thinking about death and where I would go when I died. I assumed, I would end up in heaven, though I didn't know why or how. I just figured that I was a pretty good fellow and God certainly wouldn't throw anybody like me into hell. I never did anything wrong according to what I thought.

My brother was working at Royal Fork on the weekends and playing Football in Vermilion during the week, so I didn't see him very much. One day, while we were eating at Royal Fork, Ryan explained to me that I was no better of a person than Charles Manson, the great murderer, because we all were sinners in the eyes of God. He said that it was not just the sins I had committed that would send me to hell, but that God saw the sins in my heart as well. This really bothered me because throughout the entire course of my life, I had never heard that before. I told myself this couldn't be true, because I had lived a pretty good life.

Throughout our conversation, I became more and more convicted. For the first time in my life, I was hearing the true Gospel, and God began to work on my heart. Finally, I agreed to go to church with him, even though I hadn't been to any church for five or six years.

As I sat in my brother's church that Sunday and listened to the preaching, my heart became very heavy with sorrow. It was because of what God says in the Bible about man's condition. It was at this time when I knew for sure that heaven wasn't my home.

> *Jesus answered and said unto him, Verily, verily I*
> *say unto thee, except a man be born again, he*
> *cannot see the kingdom of God.* (Jn. 3:3)

There was something inside of me that was not good and I knew it without a shadow of doubt. Even though I was not a religious person, it didn't take me long to realize that I was not right with God. From that point on, it was only a matter of time before I had to get this matter taken care of.

The next Sunday, I also went to church and was convinced even more of my condition before God, but I couldn't get over that fact that I wasn't in control.

I had already been shown through the Bible how to be saved, but for some reason I couldn't do it. Of course, I could have just prayed a prayer and got everyone off my back, but I knew I wouldn't have meant it with my heart. Besides, God could not be fooled.

During this inner struggle, God showed me that it was pride that was keeping me from Him. I was the type of person that would not bow down to any man or thing. I never had needed any so-called God. I was self-sufficient. But pride is not worth Hell-fire.

One Monday night, after having heard preaching all day Sunday, the proud barrier broke. Right then, while lying in bed, I bowed my heart to the Lord Jesus Christ and called on

Him to be my Saviour and forgive me of my sin. The moment, I did that, I knew something had happened. There was a great burden lifted and I now knew where I would spend eternity.

SHARON SMITH

Although I believed that there was a God, I never saw him as my God. I was raised in a Catholic home and went to Catholic schools most of my life. Their Easter ceremony really caused me to dislike the church, so after finishing High School, I stopped going on a regular basis.

I later got married, had a son, a good job and was doing quite well. One day a co-worker of mine asked if my son could go to a Christian Program at a Baptist church. She wanted him to go and be in the same class as her son so her son wouldn't be there without someone he knew. Wouldn't do any harm, I thought, so I said, "Sure".

One of the requirements for my son getting a uniform vest was to go to Sunday School three times in a row. There was no way I would let some church brainwash my son, so I went to see what was being taught.

While my son was in his Sunday School class, I went to the adult class. Every time I went, the preacher preached the gospel. It must have been apparent that I was lost as a goose in a snowstorm.

We went for three Sundays in a row, but never attended the main service or any other Bible study classes. Each time we went, the preacher would ask me if I would like to attend the Bible study, and each time, I politely declined. Yet, the whole time, the Lord was working on my heart and I had many questions about everything. It was all so new and different than anything that I had been taught while growing-up. The Bible was actually being used as a guide to learn about

God, instead of the books that other churches had.

Finally, I was so confused that I decided to start going to the main services to find out what it was that made my heart so heavy.

I remember hearing a message about how we were all sinners. *"For all have sinned and come short of the glory of God."* (Romans 3:23). The preacher reminded us that All meant All. I had never really seen myself as a sinner until then. I knew that I had done some really wrong things, but I had never considered them sins against God. It sure was a wake-up call for me. The preacher then told us that, *"God commendeth his love toward us, in that, while we were yet sinners, Christ died for us."* (Rom 5:8)

For the first time in my life John 3:16 made sense to me.

> *For God so loved the word, that he gave his only*
> *begotten Son, that whosoever believeth in him*
> *should not perish, but have everlasting life.*

Jesus had died for MY sins. During the invitation, the preacher said that we weren't there by mistake, but that we were there by Divine appointment. I knew that God was calling me to come to Him. Although I had tears in my eyes, my heart was crying even louder. I begged God to forgive me of my sin and save my soul from eternal damnation. I wanted Jesus in my heart and I wanted to live my life for Him.

KURT SMITH

God used a 3 year old boy to bring me to salvation.

I came from a fairly religious family and considered myself a man of honor.   I had done some good things as a husband, Father, son and son-in-law, brother and friend. I felt I was beyond reproach. I thought that God would be honored to have a great guy like ME. I sure found out I was wrong.

My wife had started to attend a Baptist church and my oldest son was in an Awana program. He had to memorize Bible verses for credit towards his uniform badges. As a good father, I naturally helped him.

One day he was practicing and came to the verse Romans 3:23, *"For all have sinned, and come short of the glory of God;"* I asked who that meant. My son included his dad, ME! In the next verse *"While we were yet sinners, Christ died for us."* (Rom 5:8) Again, when I asked who this verse included, he responded with ME, his dad. I thought, "But I'm not a sinner. I'm as perfect as a person could be. I don't need any help to go to Heaven."

My son was telling me that I was a sinner going to Hell! How dare he!   I was a good man. I did many good things and told the truth, whenever it was possible. What else did I need to do?

After much pleading from my wife, I finally went to church. There the preacher further showed me, through the preaching of the Bible, that I was lost. In his message, he pointed out that there was only one way to Heaven (John 14:6).

It was only by grace that one could be saved, not works. (Ephesians 2:8,9). In the end, he showed what would happen to those who think their WORKS would save them.

> *Not everyone that saith unto me, Lord, Lord, shall*
> *enter into the kingdom of heaven; but he that*
> *doeth the will of my Father which is in Heaven.*
> *Many will say to me in that day, Lord, Lord, have*
> *we not prophesied in thy name? and in thy name*
> *have cast out devils? and in thy name done many*
> *wonderful works? And then will I profess unto*
> *them, I never knew you: depart from me, ye that*
> *work iniquity.* (Matt 7:21-23).

That is when I knew I was a sinner on the road to Hell. During the invitation, I was asked where I would spend eternity? According to the Bible, the only answer was Hell. At that time, right at that spot, I asked Jesus Christ to come into my heart and save me.

Now, I am a sinner on the road to Heaven. What a glorious difference!

TINA STEPPAN

From the age of five until I was fifteen, I had attended three different types of churches, though not on a regular basis. My family was not religious, by any means, so I had no comprehension of what church was about or why people even went. But when I did go, I enjoyed it. The songs were fun to sing and when I memorized two Bible verses each week, I would get a prize. Vacation Bible School was fun too, because I got to learn how to make different projects.

At fifteen, I stopped attending any kind of church because of being embarrassed of the situation in our home. One day after school, I was picked up by a police officer and taken to the courthouse. There I met my mom and a friend of hers. I was told that charges were being brought against my dad for the abuse that was going on in our home, and I was being sent to live with someone else.

At that point, I felt lost and without hope, as if there was not a friend in the world that could understand the devastation and loss that I was feeling.

As an escape, I started listening to music. I was used to Country/Western, but turned to Gospel music. I can't explain what made me turn to music as my escape, from the people and problems around me, except that it brought comfort to my heavy heart.

After a few years, God led in such a way that I was put in a home where the family was faithful to God. It was not luck, but God who placed me there, because I was supposed to go back to the support group home that I came from. But God, heard my despairing cry.

After about a year of going to church with this family and listening to their conversations with other church people, the Truth of God's Word began to sink in. I did not understand that it didn't really matter how good or bad I was, so I compared myself with drinkers, smokers, and murderers. But the Bible says, *"If we say that we have no sin, we deceive ourselves, and the truth is not in us."* (I John 1:8).

I didn't realize that I needed to get saved and that I was on my way to Hell. I felt that I was the victim, not the bad guy.

The songs and verses I had heard so many times, now began to work in my heart.

> *I hear the Saviour say, Thy strength indeed is small, child of weakness watch and pray, find in Me thine all in all.*

> *Softly and tenderly Jesus is calling, calling for you and for me. . . . Come home, come home, ye who are weary, come home.*

Over the next few weeks, the Lord started showing me my sinfulness through my being deceitful and only telling half-truths. That week, on my way to school, something inside of me told me that if I died that day I would go to hell. It was God speaking to my heart. I told myself that I hadn't done anything wrong and brushed the thought off.

Then one day, I had a struggle with the lady of the home that I was staying at. The next morning, God met me in my car on the way to school and smote my heart. I asked, "What should I do?" God answered me with a Bible verse:

> *That if thou shalt confess with thy mouth the Lord Jesus, and shalt believe in thine heart that God hath raised him from the dead, thou shalt be saved. For with the heart*

> *man believeth unto righteousness and with the mouth*
> *confession is made unto salvation.* (Romans 10:9,10)

I didn't understand all that there was to know, but at that point, I realized that I was a sinner and that I would go to Hell because I was wrong. In God's sight, I was no better than the worst criminal. As I was going down the road in my car, I bowed my heart and asked God to save me.

Oh, the joy that came into my heart and the spring that was now in my steps. God Almighty had saved my soul!!

> *With my sins forgiven I am bound for Heaven, never*
> *more to roam.*

TWILA TENCLAY

I came from a family who has been in the Reformed Church in America for generations. My Father was a minister. My mother was a pastor's daughter and there were uncles on both sides who were pastors in the Reformed Church. I was raised thoroughly Calvinistic.

While I was growing up, the one doctrine that stuck in my mind was the Doctrine of Election. What if I wasn't one of the "elected?" I would go to Hell. I didn't want that and remember praying several times that God would save me from Hell. But nothing changed. Later, I went on to one of the Reformed Church colleges and took their Bible courses, but the issue of election remained unsolved in my heart.

After college, I attended a Pentecostal Church in the town where I taught school in Nebraska. Later, I moved to another town in Nebraska, and attended an Evangelical Covenant Church and put election out of my mind. Later, I moved to Albany, NY and worked in a Reformed Church and the issue of election came back full force.

I was twenty-six and still searching for God. In 1982, I moved back to the Midwest and found a job at McCrossan Boy's Ranch in Sioux Falls, SD. It was there that the Lord worked in my life to lead me to Him. The person who hired me was a Christian who belonged to Empire Baptist Temple. He was my immediate supervisor.

One of the requirements at the Ranch was that the residents had to attend church. Since the Baptist Church was the closest to what I thought I believed, I took the boys there.

My cottage partner also attended Empire Baptist and spoke highly of the pastor. We often had conversations about religion and salvation. Sometimes when our supervisor was around he would join us.

I started attending Empire Baptist Temple on the nights I was off duty. By hearing the preaching from the Bible, I had a lot of questions concerning the differences in the beliefs in which I was raised and those of this church. My supervisor and his wife were patient in answering my questions.

One Wednesday night after the evening service, I knew I needed to be saved. My supervisor's wife showed me step by step how to be saved and why I needed to be saved. Then I finally realized that I was a sinner through and through. I repented and asked the Lord to save me and He did!

I was later baptized and was so excited. I was amazed at how I knew, without question, that I was saved. There was a deep assurance that God had saved me and I knew it. No longer any doubt and wondering if I was chosen or not. I WAS!!

STEVE WILLIS

My family was not religious by any means. My father was a truck driver and gone a lot, so my mother had to carry the load of raising four children.

God used many things in my life to lead me to Him. From a young age, I knew what it was to feel alone. When I was about five, I was run over by a truck. A year or so later, my mom had a nervous breakdown. My brothers and sister and I were put into a children's home for about 10 months. When we came home there was much strife and confusion. This led my mother to alcohol. Us children were many times just left on our own, while mom worked or was at a bar.

Yet, in the midst of this turmoil, my mother sent me to a Nazarene church during a part of my childhood. There I learned about God and the Bible. My brothers and sister and I also went to a Baptist church while we were in the children's home. God was preparing my heart.

When I was in my teens, my parents ended up getting a divorce. I had little if no guidance at this time in my life.

Around the age of seventeen, a friend invited me to go on a youth outing with teens from a Baptist Church. We were going to go to New Mexico for a few days. I thought it would be great and was excited to go. But it wasn't like I thought it would be. There was a lot of preaching and it was getting under my skin.

We all had to help with chores and on the second night there, my friend, Jim and I had to do the dishes. I was frustrated, since I would rather have been outside playing with the others.   There was one man who stayed inside and was reading as far as I could tell. I felt he was going to talk to me about God and the Bible, so I tried not to pay attention to him.

Jim was washing, so he was done first and ran out the door. I still had a lot of drying to do so I kept working. The more I thought about the man being there, the more nervous I got. Finally, I was done and was walking out when he called my name. My heart dropped as I answered. Now, I would have to talk to him. I went over and sat down.

He kindly asked me what I knew about God. Nervously, I said, "God is love." He then asked me if I knew that God is holy and without sin.   He explained to me that God, who has no sin, cannot have sin in His presence.

Then he showed me verses like Romans 3:10 and 6:23
"There is none righteous, no not one."
"For the wages of sin is death; but the gift of God is eternal life through Jesus Christ our Lord."

God began to convict me. He showed me not only that I had sinned, but that my heart was full of sin and I was separated from God. He showed me that all I could do was sin.

I began to tremble heavily as I realized the gravity of the situation and the Holy Spirit convicted me of God's Truth. I felt that the ground would open and I would fall straight into Hell. I knew that God was completely just and righteous to send me to Hell. When the man asked me where I would go if I died, I said "Hell", because I knew that I was on my way there.

The man then shared verses with me about the wonderful Gift of God in Christ Jesus.

"But the gift of God is eternal life through Jesus Christ the Lord" (Rom 5:8).

He asked,

"Do you want to get saved?"

"I don't know how." I told him.

"I'll help you." He said. "Just repeat in your heart the prayer that I say."

He then began to pray, and I followed after him. Though my mouth was only repeating words from another person, my heart was crying out to God to save me. He did!

It was as if my heart exploded with a peace and warmth I had never had before, and immediately the burden of sin was lifted off my shoulders. I then knew that I was saved, but couldn't for the life of me explain it.

I told the man thanks and went outside to play. The other teens came up to me and asked what happened. I told them that I just got saved, but I was so awed by it, I really couldn't play.

Praise the Lord I had to wash dishes that night!

SHARON ALLEN

My new life began with a series of open doors. I was twenty-four, married and had a daughter. It was May of 1973, a man knocked on my door one day and shoved a paper-back Bible in my hand and ran. He didn't even say to read it or anything, but I felt the need to read it. As I began to read it, God started to convict me of my need of Him.

Next, a couple of ladies from a Baptist church came knocking on my door. They invited my daughter to ride the Sunday School bus. She was only five at the time so I thought I would go with her.

I continued to go to church until, finally one night there was a knock on my door.   It was a couple from the church I was attending. I invited them in and they witnessed to me, hoping I would want to be saved. I told them, I already knew about the Lord and they left.

But the Lord, never left me. He was there every day confronting me and letting me know that there NEVER was a time that I had received Him as my Saviour. He made me miserable, day and night. By the end of the week, I knew I needed to get saved and was ready to let God have His way. That Sunday, after the pastor preached, he asked that anyone who wanted to get saved would come to the front. I literally ran forward during the invitation. I couldn't wait any longer to get saved .

The pastor's wife dealt with me and showed me from the Bible that even good people are sinners and need to have a time when they are born again.   That day, May 23, 1973, I received Jesus into my heart and was born-again.

I was just like Nicodemus, religious and good, yet I still needed to be saved in order to go to Heaven.

"Jesus answered and said unto him,   Verily, verily   I say unto thee, except a man be born again, he cannot see the kingdom of God. " (John 3:3)

ROBERT BRANSON

Our family was like the gypsies. We never stayed in one place very long and was always on the move. Two years was usually the longest we were in any place.

At one of the places we were at, my older brother had been going to a religious group and in his zeal had "led me to the Lord". He even baptized me in our swimming pool.

Soon we moved and headed towards Canada. We didn't get there, but ended up in Washington, IN. I was twelve at the time and we started going to church, but I really didn't care about church or God then.

Later we moved to Sioux Falls, SD. There we began attending Bible Baptist church which later became, Empire Baptist Temple.

After two years, they opened a school and I started to attend it. I was a teenager at the time and I still did not have any interest in God.

One day, the Preacher took each student aside and talked to them about what they wanted to do with their life. When he talked to me, he asked about my salvation. I told him about when my brother had led me to the Lord. He then began to tell me about salvation and what it really is. A struggle in my heart began. It was as if there was a tug of war and my heart was going to break. This was the first time I realized my position before God. I saw what a sinner I was and that I was on my way to hell. I could hardly wait till the Preacher was done talking so I could get saved.

I was under so much conviction that there was a puddle of tears on the floor. I prayed and asked for forgiveness and for God to save me. Immediately, the tug of war ceased and I had peace. Now, I knew, I was saved. God then put a desire in my heart for the things of God.

God's Plan
Of
Salvation

"For God so loved the world that He gave his only begotten son that whosoever believeth in him should not perish, but have everlasting life."
John 3:16

"The Lord is not slack concerning his promise, as some men count slackness; but is longsuffering to us-ward, not willing that any should perish, but that all should come to repentance."
I Peter 3:9

ALL ROADS LEAD TO ROME

When Rome was in power, it was the center of everything in that part of the world. Commerce, religion, and business, was controlled by the strength of Rome. Cities and towns were built around Rome and roads were directed towards this great city. This is where the term "All Roads lead to Rome" came from. In those days, any road, in that part of the world, did eventually lead to Rome.

Now, this term is taken to apply to religion. There are many different religions in the world today, who's to say which is right and which are wrong? We all have our own opinion and one person's opinion is just as good as another's. So "All Roads lead to Rome," right? After all, we're all trying to reach that Great City, Heaven.

Some hold that this view applies to all forms of Christianity, and others believe it is for all religions and those who do good. However there are some serious problems with this concept.

HEAVEN IS GOD'S CITY

If some stranger were to come to your house and just walk right in, and act as if it belonged to him, what would you do? Would it not be an offense to you? Does anyone have the right to come into your home uninvited and demand that he be allowed to live there? Yet, many do this with God. They impose their rules for entering Heaven on God, yet fail to realize that . . . .

Heaven belongs to God!

He made it! He owns it! He makes the rules! We cannot get there on our own, nor do we have any right to say who is allowed in its doors. No human being does. Our job is to find out what God's rules are. This is found in the Bible.

In a way the phrase, *All Roads Lead to Rome*, is right. It is true that there are many religions and though they disagree in some areas, they do agree in others. The only problem is that their destination is not Heaven, but HELL. Remember, most religions are man-made, man-centered and man-gratifying. Even Jesus and the Apostle's greatest enemies were the religious leaders of their day.

God says that the way to Heaven is narrow and FEW will find it. Are you one of the few on the way to Heaven, or one of the many that will end up in Hell?

> *Enter ye in at the strait gate: for wide is the gate, and*
> *broad is the way, that leadeth to destruction, and*
> *many there be which go in thereat; because strait is*
> *the gate, and narrow is the way, which leadeth unto*
> *life, and few there be that find it.* (Matt. 7:14)

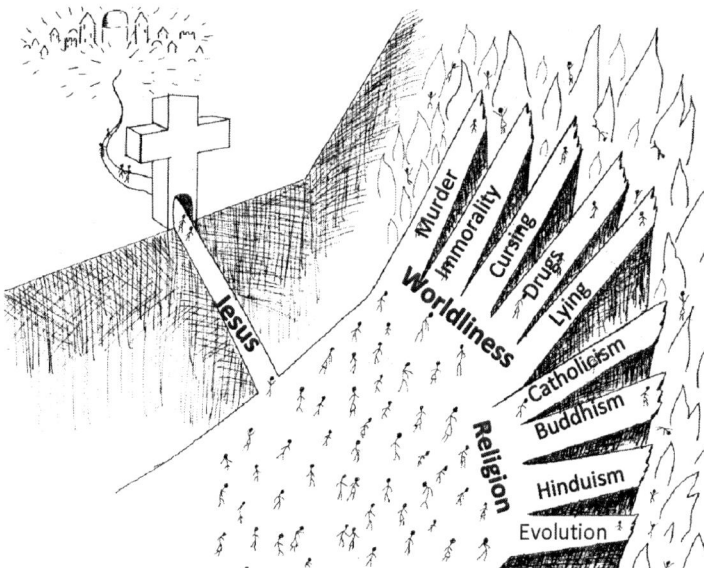

THE 10 COMMANDMENTS

God has given us His Ten Commandments to show us what His standard is:

I. Thou shalt have no other Gods before me.
II. Thou shalt not make any graven image nor bow down to them.
III. Thou shalt not take the name of The Lord thy God in vain.
IV. Remember the Sabbath day and keep it holy.
V. Honor thy Father and Mother
VI. Thou shalt not kill
VII. Thou shalt not commit adultery
VIII. Thou shalt not steal
IX. Thou shalt not bear false witness
X. Thou shalt not covet

I	VI
II	VII
III	VIII
IV	IX
V	X

How do YOU stand? Let us take the ninth commandment, *"Thou shalt not bear false witness."* Have you ever lied? If we are honest, we would admit that we have lied, probably more times than we would like to say. According to one study, the average person in America, lies 7 times a day. This does sound like a lot, but sometimes we lie not even realizing it. God hates lying and will punish all those who lie. In Revelations 21: 8 it states,

> But the fearful, and unbelieving, and the abominable, and murderers, and whoremongers, and sorcerers, and idolaters, and <u>all liars,</u> shall have their part in the lake which burneth with fire and brimstone: which is the second death.

What about the third commandment, *"Thou shalt not take the name of the Lord thy God in vain."* God's name is commonly used as a cuss word, yet few seem to think much of it. This is a serious crime against God almighty, and it is called blasphemy. God required death for this sin (Mark 14:64). Not only will we be judged for taking God's name in vain, we will also be judged for every word we speak. Jesus said,

> *But I say unto you, That every idle word that men shall speak, they shall give account thereof in the day of judgment.* (Matthew 12:36).

Think on this a little. Everything that you have said, throughout your entire life, will be judged by a holy and righteous God. It has been recorded.

The sixth commandment is, *"Thou shalt not kill."* We may think that we have not done this, but listen to what Jesus says,

> *Ye have heard that it was said by them of old time, thou shalt not kill; and whosoever shall kill shall be in danger of the judgment: But I say unto you, That whosoever is angry with his brother without a cause shall be in danger of the judgment: and whosoever shall say to his brother, Raca, shall be in danger of the council: but whosoever shall say, Thou fool, shall be in danger of hell fire.* (Matthew 5:21,22)

How do you stand? How we treat others is important in God's eyes.

What about the seventh commandment, *"Thou shalt not commit adultery"*? Perhaps, you have not been guilty of this, but Jesus explains God's righteous standard even further.

> *Ye have heard that it was said by them of old time, thou shalt not commit adultery: But I say unto you, that whosoever looketh on a woman to lust after her hath*

committed adultery with her already in his heart." (Matt. 5:27,28)

God further says in Hebrews 13:4, "*Marriage is honourable in all, and the bed undefiled: but whoremongers and adulterers God will judge.*" God's standard is holy. He does not allow any type of sexual activity or thoughts outside of marriage between one man and one woman.

What about the last commandment, "Thou shalt not covet"? Webster's Dictionary defines covet as, "to desire inordinately; to desire that which is unlawful to obtain." The Bible further states that to covet is like idolatry and that no one who does so will enter Heaven. *For this ye know, that no whoremonger, nor unclean person, covetous man, who is an idolater hath any inheritance in the kingdom of Christ and of God.* (Ephesians 5:5).

This is only 5 of the 10 commandments, but what about the commandments that deal with our relationship with God. We are not to have any other God beside the Lord God of Heaven, the Creator of the universe, and we are not to bow down or serve any idol. Have you not failed here? Have you not put something or someone as more important than God and His Holy Word, thus committing idolatry?

God has a holy standard for those who would enter Heaven, and He does not want us to be deceived by any man or religion that says otherwise.

> *Know ye not that the unrighteous shall not inherit the kingdom of God? Be not deceived; nether fornicators, nor idolaters, nor adulterers, nor effeminate, nor abusers of themselves with mankind, nor thieves, nor covetous, nor drunkards, nor revilers, nor extortioners, shall inherit the kingdom of God.* (I Corinthians 6:9,10).

We may think that maybe we have only broken 3 of the ten commandments, so we should be alright. Yet, the Bible says otherwise. Whether we have broken one or all of the commandments of God, we are still guilty before God. This is because God's law is like a chain. Every link is important, and it only takes one link to be broken for the chain to be broken. Even so, when we break one of the commandments of God, we are guilty of all. *"For whosoever shall keep the whole law, and yet offend in one point, he is guilty of all."* (James 2:10).

GOD'S JUDGMENT

God's holy and righteous law proves all of us to be guilty and in danger of Judgment.

> *Now we know that what things soever the law saith, it saith to them who are under the law: that every mouth may be stopped, and all the world may become guilty before God.* (Romans 3:19)

God almighty has declared that, "There is none righteous, no not one," and that "All have sinned and come short of the glory of God." Then He pronounces, that *"As it is appointed unto men once to die, but after this the judgment."* (Hebrews 9:27). God does have something to say about this judgment that we all will face:

> *But we are sure that the judgment of God is according to truth against them which commit such things [the breaking of God's laws] And thinkest thou this, O man, that judgest them which do such things, and doest the same, that thou shalt escape the judgment of God? But after thy hardness and impenitent heart treasurest up unto thyself wrath against the day of wrath and revelation of the righteous judgment of God;* (Romans 2:2,3,5)

For we must all appear before the judgment seat of Christ; that every one may receive the things done in his body, according to that he hath done, whether it be good or bad. (II Corinthians 5:10)

But the heavens and the earth, which are now, by the same word are kept in store, reserved unto fire against the day of judgment and perdition of ungodly men. (II Peter 2:7)

To execute judgment upon all, and to convince all that are ungodly among them of all their ungodly deeds which they have ungodly committed, and of all their hard speeches which ungodly sinners have spoken against him [God]. (Jude 1:5)

God's judgment is that we would be thrown into HELL. Did you know that Jesus spoke more about hell than heaven? He must have thought that it was pretty important for us to know about. Here are some verses from the Bible about Hell.

And fear not them which kill the body, but are not able to kill the soul: but rather fear him which is able to destroy both soul and body in hell. (Matthew 10:28)

Then shall he say also unto them on the left hand, Depart from me, ye cursed, into everlasting fire, prepared for the devil and his angels: (Matt 25:41)

And these shall go away into everlasting punishment: but the righteous into life eternal. (Matt 25:46)

And shall cast them into a furnace of fire: there shall be wailing and gnashing of teeth. (Matt 13:42)

> *And the smoke of their torment ascendeth up for ever and ever: and they have no rest day nor night,... (Rev. 14:11)*

> *And if thy hand offend thee, cut it off: it is better for thee to enter into life maimed, than having two hands to go into hell, into the fire that never shall be quenched:* (Mark 9:28)

> *But I will forewarn you whom ye shall fear: Fear him, which after he hath killed hath power to cast into hell; yea, I say unto you, Fear him.* (Luke 12 :5)

Mankind is hanging over the flames of hell, doomed to burn. The thin thread of life, by which they hang, is constantly threatened to break – any instance. Once broken, they will plunge into a furnace of fire, and be tormented day and night, with no hope of any relief ***forever***, and ***forever,*** and ***FOREVER***.

At this point, if you realize that you are headed straight for hell, with no way of escaping, you may go to page 61, section: God's Simple Plan of Salvation. Otherwise, read on, until you see the grave situation you are in.

GOOD WORKS WILL NOT SAVE

Many think that their good will be weighed against their bad and because they have done a lot of good, it would certainly out-weigh the bad. Of course, God being so good, He would overlook the bad and let them into Heaven. After all God is good and you're really a decent person, there's no way He'd send you to hell.

There are some problems with this concept. Let's take a man convicted of a crime, rape, murder, or theft. He is caught and brought before a judge and duly convicted. The judge then says,

"You are guilty and I will now pronounce your sentence. Do you have anything to say?"

"Yes, your honor," the convict confidently states, "I know you're a good judge, and that you'll overlook the wrong that I did, because I have done a lot of good in my life time." He continues to tell the judge of all the nice things he has done. "I am a decent person. I've given to charity, I was baptized when I was young, I helped others ....."

Would any good judge let the criminal go? No, and neither will God, but because He is good, justice must be served. He will punish sin and He will not pardon us based on any good that we have done. ALL sin will be punished.

This is what God says about our "goodness".

But we are all as an unclean [thing], and all our <u>*righteousnesses are as filthy rags;*</u> *and we all do fade as a leaf; and our iniquities, like the wind, have taken us away.* (Isaiah 64:6)

Before God our righteousness or goodness is filthy! Yes, filthy, like a rag that you just cleaned the toilet with. This is why God stated:

Therefore by the deeds of the law there shall no flesh be justified in his sight: for by the law is the knowledge of sin. (Romans 3:20)

The law that this is talking about is not only the moral law of God as is seen in the 10 commandments, but all the religious laws that the Jews had. These religious customs and rituals will not take man's sin away. The purpose of the law, was to show mankind their sinfulness before a holy God. Nothing in the law could bring about salvation of the soul. Not baptism, tithing, church membership or attendance, helping others, volunteering, taking the sacraments, or any other righteous or religious work will get anyone into Heaven.

We must realize that it will be by the standard set forth in the Word of God that we will be judged; therefore, it is important that we know what the Bible says about our eternity. Let us examine from the Bible what God has to say about the common salvation methods used.

RELIGION WILL NOT SAVE

Baptism - Many Christian religions claim that one must be baptized and that this is necessary for the salvation of the soul. Yet, what does the Bible say about this.

There are two key verses used to prove that baptism is necessary for salvation. The first one is:
John 3:5

> *Jesus saith unto him, verily, verily I say unto you, Except a man be born of water and of the spirit, he cannot enter the kingdom of heaven.*

To rightly understand any verse in the Bible, it must be evaluated according to its context. At the beginning of the chapter, it is told how Nicodemus came to Jesus at night and Jesus talked to him. Jesus then said, that "except a man be born again, he cannot enter the kingdom of heaven." Nicodemus then said to Jesus, "How can a man be born when he is old? Can he enter the second time into his mother's womb, and be born?" To this Jesus answered, that *"except a man be born of water and of the spirit, he cannot enter the kingdom of heaven."*

Jesus is clearly talking about being born from one's mother's womb that Nicodemus just mentioned. This is being born of water. In the womb, a baby is protected by a bag of water, when this bag breaks, then the baby is born. Jesus is comparing being born of the flesh, from the mother's womb, with being born of the Spirit of God.

Right after this verse, Jesus then state, *"That which is born of the flesh, is flesh; and that which is born of the spirit is spirit."* Vs 6

It is clear from the context that there is nothing in this passage that indicates that baptism is necessary for salvation or even that baptism has any part in salvation.

The second verse that is used to teach that baptism has a part in salvation is:

I Peter 3:21*"The like figure where unto even Baptism doth also now save us (not the putting away of the filth of the flesh, but the answer of a good conscience toward God,) by the resurrection of Jesus Christ:"*

Again, the context of this verse is very important in order to accurately understand it. What does the "like figure" refer to in this verse? The verse before this states,

"Which sometime were disobedient, when once the longsuffering of God waited in the days of Noah, while the ark was a preparing, wherein few, that is, eight souls were saved by water."

The "like figure" is talking about the eight souls in Noah's ark (Noah, his three sons, and their wives), that were saved *by water.* Yes, they were saved by the water, but the only reason why was because they were in the Ark. Everyone

else who was not in the Ark, drowned. The water saved Noah and his family in that it buoyed the Ark up above the water.

This is the figure that verse 21 is referring to. This is why to clarify what is meant, in parenthesis it says, "(not the putting away of the filth of the flesh, but the answer of a good conscience toward God)" Water baptism is as the waters in Noah's flood, and the Ark represents Jesus Christ. Baptism will no more save anyone than the waters in Noah's flood saved anyone other than those within the Ark. In fact, the waters brought death to those who were not in the Ark, so will baptism bring eternal damnation to those who have not been born again and trust in it, instead of the finished work of Christ in salvation

Baptizing Babies

The practice of baptizing babies comes from Romans 16:33. Paul was in prison and an earthquake shook loose the chains of the prisoners. The keeper was about to kill himself, when Paul stopped him. He then came to Paul and asked what he must do to be saved. *Paul answered, "Believe on the Lord Jesus Christ, and thou shalt be saved, and thy house."* And they spoke to him and those in his house the word of the Lord and in verse 33 it states that, he "was baptized, he and all his, straightway."

Yet, nowhere in the passage does it say that there were any children in this house, but those who hold to infant baptism claim that there must have been children. Yet, the Bible does not say this. Is this not adding to the Word of God?

Furthermore, one of the Biblical qualifications of baptism is to believe on the Jesus Christ for salvation. This is clear in Acts 8:36,37. Philip preached Jesus to an Ethiopian, who when they were passing by some water said, *"See here is water; what doth hinder me to be baptized? And Philip said, If thou believest with all thine heart, thou mayest. And he answered and said, I believe that Jesus Christ is the Son of God."* Then he was baptized. Any baby or child that does not have enough understanding to believe on Jesus Christ for salvation does not even qualify for Scriptural baptism. This is very clear in the Bible.

The Sacraments or Communion

There are those who hold to religious teachings that taking the sacraments or Holy Communion will wash away one's sins. This cannot be found in the Bible.

Jesus gave the communion as a remembrance for his disciples. It did not take away their sin, and nowhere is there any indication in the Bible that taking the communion could wash away sin.

Some claim that the bread and the wine are literally Jesus's body and blood, and that by partaking of it, one's sins are washed away. This thought comes from where Jesus says, "This IS my body . . . This IS my blood . . . " This teaching is inaccurate for several reasons. One, is that at the time Jesus gave the first communion, He had not even yet died nor shed his blood. It is clearly symbolic of the sacrifice he was about to make as the Lamb of God.

Secondly, in several ways God uses comparisons to help us understand more clearly. Here are a few. Jesus said, "I am the door..." John 10:7,9. We clearly understand that this does not mean that He is a literal door, but that He represents that door in which one must go through in order to enter Heaven. Another example is that Jesus is called the Lamb of God. This does not mean that He is an animal, but that He fills the position as a sacrificial Lamb. (Jn 1:29,36; Rev. 19:9; 21:22,23; 22:1,3). In the Old Testament, God said, "I am thy shield...." (Gen 15:1). This represents that God protects us, not that He is a literal shield.

The main reason why the belief that partaking of the communion will wash away our sin, or that it has any part in salvation, is wrong, is because the Bible says nothing about this concept. Here are the passages in the Bible about communion. We recommend that you thoroughly study them, and then you will understand that the practice of communion is for us to remember Jesus Christ's death, and is not a means of salvation. (I Cor. 11:25; Luke 22:17; Mark 14:23; Matthew 26:27).

Not By Works

If we could earn our way to heaven by ourselves through good works or religion, why then would Jesus have had to come to die for our sins? Even in the garden of Gethsemane, Jesus prayed and cried, *"If it be possible, let this*

A New Life

cup pass from me:" (Matt. 26:39).   Only because it is NOT possible for man to earn his way to Heaven did Jesus have to go to the cross and bear our sins. Would the God of the universe, the Creator of all, subject Himself to suffer needlessly?

> *Not by works of righteousness which we have done,*
> *but according to his mercy he saved us, by the*
> *washing of regeneration, and renewing of the Holy*
> *Ghost.* (Titus 3:5).

The Thief on the Cross

When Jesus was on the cross, there were two thieves hanging on crosses as well. One on his right, and the other on his left. One of them spoke harshly to Jesus, demanding Him to save them. The other rebuked him, and admitted that they were receiving justice for the wrong that they had done, but that Jesus had done nothing wrong. He then said to Jesus, "Lord, remember me when thou comest into thy kingdom." Jesus answered, *"Today shalt thou be with me in paradise."* (Luke 23:39:43).   No baptism, no communion, and no good works. What did this criminal do that he would be allowed to enter paradise?

THE WORK OF SALVATION

There were those who came to Jesus and asked him, *"What shall we do, that we might work the works of God?"* To this Jesus answered and said unto them, *"This is the work of God, that ye believe on him whom he hath sent."* (John 6:28,29)

This is what God requires of all mankind. The faith and belief in this verse is not a casual "believe", but casting our entire confidence for the salvation of our soul on Jesus Christ.

There is as story about a famous tight rope walker that crossed Niagara falls on a tight-rope. He printed in the local paper that he would walk across the falls with a wheel barrel full of rocks.

55

The day came and the crowd was big and excited about the event. The man came out with his wheel barrel and asked, "How many of you believe that I can make it across the tight rope and back?" The crowd cheered loudly and said, "We believe you can do it." He got on the tight-rope and made it to the other side and back with the wheel barrel full of rocks.

The crowd thundered with cheers. The man said, "How many of you believe I can push a man or woman in my wheel barrel across and back?" The crowd got even more excited and cheered. Then, he asked for a volunteer. He wanted someone to get into the wheelbarrow, and let him carry him across. No one volunteered. No one trusted him enough to put their lives in his hands.

Many are like the crowd who cheer that they "believe", yet have not turned to God in repentance and Faith in Jesus Christ alone for the salvation of their soul. Repentance and total commitment and trust in Jesus Christ and His finished work on the cross is what God requires.

GOD'S SIMPLE PLAN OF SALVATION

God saw mankind's awful dilemma, and reached down to recue us. God's plan of salvation is as simple as A, B, C.

Admit

Believe

Confess

<u>Admit</u> One must first admit his condition before God. You must realize that you are a sinner headed straight for Hell. Admit the truth of what God says about yourself.

"As it is written, there is none righteous, no, not one.
For all have sinned and come short of the Glory of God."
(Romans 3:10,23).

<u>Believe</u> The Biblical meaning of Believe is: to trust; to fully depend on; to have full persuasion of. The message throughout the Bible is that salvation is through believing what God says about ourselves, and then placing our trust on the finished work of Jesus Christ.

Jesus Christ was God incarnate, the Creator of the universe. He was born into this world by a virgin through the power of the Holy Spirit of God. He grew up and never sinned in word, thought, or deed. He kept the whole commandments of God, then at the age of 30, He started preaching and teaching others.

For three and a half years, he taught and performed many miracles. These consisted of healing people of various diseases, making the blind to see, causing the lame to walk, providing food, and even raising the dead. In so much that it was said of Him, "How can a man do the things that you do, except God be with him."

Many followed him. But the religious crowd was jealous, and planned for his execution. They stirred the people up and caused him to be put to death by painful crucifixion. Yet, Jesus even knew beforehand that he would die and how and why. At the time of his death, around 3 p.m., the whole sky was dark and an earthquake occurred. In so much, that a Roman soldier centurion, declared in Mark 15:39, "Truly this man was the Son of God!"

Jesus was then buried, but it does not end there. On the third day, He rose up from the dead!! No one has ever conquered death, but only Jesus Christ, God Almighty! After rising from the dead, He met with his disciples for 40 days, and then he went up into Heaven.

This Jesus, is the one who has power over death and life; Heaven and Hell. All power is given to Him. It is this Jesus Christ, the Creator of ALL, that we are to believe and obey.

> *He that believeth on the Son hath everlasting life: and he that believeth not the Son shall not see life; but the wrath of God abideth on him. (Jn 3:36)*

"But as many as received him, to them gave he power to become the sons of God, [even] to them that believe on his name:" (Jn 1:12)

For after that in the wisdom of God the world by wisdom knew not God, it pleased God by the foolishness of preaching to save them that believe. I Cor 1:21

<u>Confess</u>   The last step is simply to confess your need before God and man. This includes repentance. Repentance is a change of mind which brings about a change of action. You must realize your sinful condition before God, and change your mind about yourself.   You must also repent from human methods and reasoning to save yourself, and accept God's way of salvation. Then you confess this change that has taken place in your heart to God and man.

That if thou shalt confess with thy mouth the Lord Jesus, and shalt believe in thine heart that God hath raised him from the dead, thou shalt be saved.

For with the heart man believeth unto righteousness, and with the mouth confession is made unto salvation.

For whosoever shall call upon the name of the Lord shall be saved. " (Romans 10:9,10,13)

This is what the Bible calls to be Born Again.

For God so loved the world that he gave his only begotten Son, that whosoever believeth on Him should not perish, but have everlasting life. (John 3:16).

> *Jesus answered and said unto him, Verily, verily, I*
> *say unto thee, except a man be born again, he cannot*
> *see the kingdom of God.* (Jn. 3:3)

* * * * * * * * * *

As in the stories in this book, the manner of prayer: when, where, and what was said, is not the main focus. The importance is always the condition of one's heart.

There is nothing on this earth more important than our soul. The longest we would live may be 80, or for a few, 100 years, but after this life is eternity. Think of that. Forever and forever and forever in Heaven or Hell. What will it be? The decision is yours and yours alone.

Remember, God is loving and merciful, but He WILL NOT be mocked. He is God. There will be a LAST CHANCE. Don't gamble with your soul.

> *He that rejecteth me, and receiveth not my words, hath*
> *one that judgeth him: the word that I have spoken, the*
> *same shall judge him in the last day.* (John 12:48)